ON COMMUNITY CIVIL DISOBEDIENCE IN THE NAME OF SUSTAINABILITY

The Community Rights Movement in the United States

Community Environmental Legal Defense Fund

PM PRESS PAMPHLET SERIES

0001: BECOMING THE MEDIA: A CRITICAL HISTORY OF CLAMOR MAGAZINE
By Jen Angel

0002: DARING TO STRUGGLE, FAILING TO WIN: THE RED ARMY FACTION'S 1977 CAMPAIGN OF DESPERATION
By J. Smith and André Moncourt

0003: MOVE INTO THE LIGHT: POSTSCRIPT TO A TURBULENT 2007
By The Turbulence Collective

0004: THE PRISON-INDUSTRIAL COMPLEX AND THE GLOBAL ECONOMY
By Eve Goldberg and Linda Evans

0005: ABOLISH RESTAURANTS: A WORKER'S CRITIQUE OF THE FOOD SERVICE INDUSTRY
By Prole

0006: SING FOR YOUR SUPPER: A DIY GUIDE TO PLAYING MUSIC, WRITING SONGS, AND BOOKING YOUR OWN GIGS
By David Rovics

0007: PRISON ROUND TRIP
By Klaus Viehmann

0008: SELF-DEFENSE FOR RADICALS: A TO Z GUIDE FOR SUBVERSIVE STRUGGLE
By Mickey Z.

0009: SOLIDARITY UNIONISM AT STARBUCKS
By Staughton Lynd and Daniel Gross

0010: COINTELSHOW: A PATRIOT ACT
By L.M. Bogad

0011: ORGANIZING COOLS THE PLANET: TOOLS AND REFLECTIONS TO NAVIGATE THE CLIMATE CRISIS
By Hilary Moore and Joshua Kahn Russell

0012: "VENCEREMOS": VÍCTOR JARA AND THE NEW CHILEAN SONG MOVEMENT
By Gabriel San Román

0013: ON COMMUNITY CIVIL DISOBEDIENCE IN THE NAME OF SUSTAINABILITY: THE COMMUNITY RIGHTS MOVEMENT IN THE UNITED STATES
By Community Environmental Legal Defense Fund

PM Press PAMPHLET SERIES No. 0013
On Community Civil Disobedience in the Name of Sustainability: The Community Rights Movement in the United States
© Community Environmental Legal Defense Fund

ISBN: 978-1-62963-126-4

Copyright © 2015

This edition copyright PM Press
All rights reserved

Layout by Jonathan Rowland

PM Press
PO Box 23912
Oakland, CA 94623
www.pmpress.org

Printed in Oakland, CA, on recycled paper with soy ink.

CONTENTS

	Introduction	1
ONE	Why Environmental and Labor Laws Protect Neither the Environment nor Workers	9
TWO	Why and How the U.S. Constitution Protects Property and Commerce	16
THREE	Energizing and Accelerating Necessary Constitutional Change	21
FOUR	Driving the Local into the State	30
FIVE	Driving the Local and the State Upward into the National	45
SIX	An Invitation	48
	Notes	50
	About CELDF	57

Introduction

"SUSTAINABILITY IS ILLEGAL UNDER OUR SYSTEM OF LAW."

I first uttered that sentence during a keynote speech I gave at a progressive conference many years ago. I can't remember which one. What I do remember is my utter frustration with conference attendees that led me to say it.

I had been trying to explain how our system of law in the United States systematically strips communities of the power to adopt and enforce local laws, when those laws come into direct conflict with decisions made by corporations that want to use those communities for various projects. And how *our system of law elevates the corporate "right" to decide, above the rights of you and me to clean air, clean water, and sustainability* in general. Which means that corporate projects of all kinds—from giant factory farms to the dumping of toxic waste—are generally exempted from the community laws that we adopt to protect our rights.

Which, of course, most people living in the United States can't hear because it directly challenges **a central myth that we've been fed all of our lives—that we actually live in a democracy where we have the ability and authority (indeed, the "right") to govern ourselves within our own communities**. Because of our belief in that myth, we have a difficult time hearing anything that doesn't fit within it.

And, of course, we *do* have the ability to self-govern in areas like how tall the weeds should be on our neighbor's lawn, or whether our local government should invest pension monies in tobacco corporations. Or whether our community can keep adult bookstores away from elementary schools. But on the really big issues—like what farming, energy production, or waste management will look like in our community—we're simply out of luck. *When "we the people" try to locally legislate in those areas—usually when a corporate factory farm or industrial wind turbine are proposed for our community—we find that we have both hands tied behind our backs.* We are then informed that **our municipal governments have no authority to interfere with decisions already made by certain corporations, and that "rights" claimed by those corporations are not only more important than our rights to clean air and clean water, but that those corporate "rights" are derived from our very own Constitution.**

What do we do then, after we are informed that our system of law leaves us powerless to contest the decision-making authority of those corporations? We try to work around the bedrock system of law—by appealing permits issued under legal frameworks designed by the very corporations that those frameworks are ostensibly supposed to regulate, and by trying to negotiate with the corporations planning those projects. In other words, **instead of questioning why corporations can legally treat our communities as sacrifice zones, we accept their authority to do so**, while attempting to make their proposed project a little less harmful.

That is, *we validate how the existing system operates by leaving it alone*—as if handed down to us from above—and we have no business challenging it. We then content ourselves to call what we have democracy.

It's a good thing that we don't live in the 1840s. Otherwise, we might leave African-Americans and women as property, while merely attempting to regulate the number of lashes a slave could receive, or mandating whether a woman's husband or brother had decision-making authority for her. In other words, we wouldn't have contested *whether* African-Americans and women were property, but simply how that property was treated under the law.

Under our current system of law, *our communities remain corporate property* by virtue of the relationship between corporate "rights" and our nonexistent ones, and more often than not, we accept our role by merely arguing over how our community is treated, rather than asserting that we have a right to decide for ourselves.

Thus, we happily content ourselves (at least for the duration of the process) by sending letters to our elected representatives, arguing over pollutant parts per million at regulatory agencies, hiring lawyers to appeal permits, and generally doing everything else but taking aim at a system of law that has divested us of almost all decision-making authority.

We do it because we're allowed to participate in certain limited ways, and because we actually believe that we live in a democracy.

A system that operates in this manner, however, is not a democracy. Instead, we have a structure of law based on giving a small handful of corporate decision-makers almost wholesale control over our communities on almost any issue that really matters.

Building economically and environmentally sustainable communities—something that our very survival on this planet depends upon—cannot be done through a system that elevates the "rights" of corporate entities driven by unsustainability, above the rights of people and communities interested in establishing a different system. Nor can it be done through a corporate culture whose primary, overriding goal is—as historian Richard L. Grossman often said—the **production of "endless more."**

Why is it that the last fifty years of activism hasn't yielded a system that understands that the *production of endless more* will destroy not only the finite resource systems on which we rely for survival, but also the quality of life of people living in communities that are exploited for that endless production? **Why hasn't our activism succeeded in building a new legal and economic system that recognizes environmental limits and enforces democratic control?**

To answer those questions, we need to critically examine the last fifty years of labor and environmental activism—*activism that has been focused almost exclusively on "working the system" rather than working to change the structure under which the system operates.*

Working the system has meant embracing a system of law that supports an unholy alliance of decision-makers, corporate and governmental, as they make decisions based on a model of unlimited growth. We've spent a lot of energy changing the elected "who," but that hasn't changed the underlying model under which we all operate.

It is because we have been unable and perhaps unwilling to see this system for what it is, and change our activism to be commensurate with the systemic problems that we face, that our activism has been ineffective—because we have continued to work *within a system that was constructed to make our activism ultimately ineffective.*

In my last breath of frustration at that conference long ago, I told the audience that **sustainability itself had been rendered illegal under our system of law and that the only organizing worth its salt—the only kind of activism that is going to save human and natural communities from environmental and economic catastrophe—was that which focused on** *making sustainability legal*. In other words, creating a system in which law enables people to legislate sustainable energy, transportation, and agricultural systems into being, rather than one that enables corporate decision-makers to mandate unsustainable systems over sustainable ones.

It didn't change much at the conference—there was head nodding by some, confused and glazed-over looks by others, but I've found the idea of *sustainability as illegal* to be useful in reaching those of the progressive or liberal ilk. That we can't get to where we need to go by working within the existing system means we must retool our activism to build a new structure of law.

Of course, sustainability *is* illegal—for the simple fact that under our system, the law *services* the overriding goal of the production of endless more—by making everything standing in the way of that endless production illegal and, in many cases, unconstitutional.

And that's a hard one for people to get under their belts—especially progressives and liberals, who believe that all we have to do is elect good people to office or work to pass nonbinding resolutions urging Congress to do this or that. Theirs is the belief that all we have to do is mobilize majorities around a given issue, and that in itself will be sufficient to move toward sustainable systems. It is that myth, unfortunately, which has held our organizing hostage over the last hundred years.

Under our system of law, you see, *it doesn't matter how many people mobilize or who we elect*—simply because the levers of law can't be directly exercised by them. And even when they do manage to swing the smallest of those levers, they get swung back (either through the legislature or the courts) by a corporate minority who claimed control over them a long time ago.

If the *legal system makes almost everything corporations do legal and constitutional*, then the only effective form of activism must be one that seeks to create a new legal and constitutional framework—one that snatches decision-making power from the "who" of today and gives it to the communities of tomorrow.

It also means understanding that *law and culture must change together*. That questioning the production of endless more automatically means questioning a system of law harnessed to it; and vice versa, questioning the way the system of law operates draws into question the basic value of what that system is intended to protect.

Others who came before us understood this dynamic—the Abolitionists understood that they lived in a "slave state" in which decisions were made by a discrete few, which was backed by an understanding that the economic system of slavery was what kept those few in power. The "who" of the 1840s had built a culture that treated slavery as a "good." In order for the Abolitionists to destroy a system of law that treated slavery as legal, they had to destroy a system of culture that treated slavery as a good. Women were in the same position—hacking away at the legal and constitutional structure while simultaneously dismantling a culture that treated women as inevitable and unquestionable second-class citizens.

We face the same dilemma today—**a *system of law* that elevates corporations (and the relatively small number of people who own and control them) above people and communities, and a *system of culture* that treats our subordinancy to those corporations as "good" and "democratic."** Our corporate culture sells that elevation of corporate "rights" above the people's rights as necessary for economic expansion and well-being.

As a people of "we the people" fame, we have become either ahistorical, amazingly obedient, exceedingly stupid, or all three. It's not just our fault, of course—billions of dollars have been spent to keep us exactly where we are. And we can stay that way if we choose—either denying that the system operates as it does or resigning ourselves to it—with the understanding that *every day we fail to challenge how the system operates is another day that the planet falls down around us*.

It's not just the corporations' prowess, either. The "founders" of the United States trusted corporate decision-makers more than they trusted people. Condemnations of democracy were rampant within the halls of the 1789 Philadelphia Constitutional Convention. Debates focused on how best to dilute democratic authority *to make sure that those who owned property could govern those who didn't.* Energies released by the American Revolution and all that it represented in terms of the power of "we the people" had to be stuffed back into the bottle from whence it came as quickly as possible.

The adults in their wigs and carriages had to stop the inmates from taking over the prison.

"It's the Constitution, stupid" hasn't come into vogue yet, but it must. We live under a 1790s system of law that is premised on the ultimate importance and protection of property—over almost all other values. It's a stark reality that while racial and other minorities still struggle for basic human rights, corporations—as pieces of property—have been provided cloaks of the highest and strongest constitutional protections. It's even starker when one considers that *corporations received core constitutional "rights" in the 1840s to 1880s, long before women were recognized as having those rights by the ratification of a federal suffrage amendment in 1920.*

And so communities attempting to use that system of constitutional law to transition toward economic and environmental sustainability run into not the threatening corporations first but rather into their own constitutional structure—with the highest pledge of that constitutional structure being to protect the production of endless more.

In response to communities crying "enough," the law replies with, *"There can never be enough."*

The challenge, thus, is to turn the system upside down—an open, direct, and frontal challenge to a system embedded in the 1700s, which is stopping us from moving into the century of sustainability. **Such an era must elevate the rights of people, communities, and nature above the "rights" currently claimed by corporations and their decision-makers.**

Such a transformation would restore the original American revolutionary concept—embedded into all of our state constitutions—that "we the people" are the source of all political authority.

Lucky for us, others seeking to force structural change have gone before. It is to those voices that we must listen to determine which activism on our part is going to make the difference before it becomes too late to make any difference at all.

Thomas Linzey, executive director
Community Environmental Legal Defense Fund
January 2015

ONE

Why Environmental and Labor Laws Protect Neither the Environment nor Workers

THE PROMISE OF ENVIRONMENTAL AND LABOR LAW
As the first decade of the new century comes to a close, humankind's impact on the natural environment is becoming ever more distressingly obvious. This past decade, we have witnessed Hurricane Katrina, the BP oil spill in the Gulf of Mexico, and the shrinking of the Arctic ice cap by nearly 30 percent. By some accounts, as much as 70 percent of all biodiversity on the planet has been lost.

To even the most casual observer, **it has become clear that we are in the midst of ecosystem collapse, which includes the destruction of our own life-support systems.** The reasons are not surprising—each year, in the United States alone, 570 billion pounds of municipal waste is produced, with 60 percent of that waste ending up in landfills or incinerators; 4 billion pounds of toxic chemicals—including 72 million pounds of known carcinogens—are released into the atmosphere from 20,000 industrial polluters; and 2 trillion pounds of livestock waste—laced with antibiotics, hormones, and chemicals—are dumped into waterways and applied to land.

Eleven million people live within one mile of a federal Superfund site. The use of fossil fuels for 85 percent of our energy use impacts the health of 6 million people in the U.S., while warming and polluting the atmosphere. Eighty thousand industrial chemicals currently are in use in the U.S., with more than 700 now found within every human body. More than 1,800 new chemicals are introduced annually.

Forty percent of our waterways fail to meet even the minimal requirements of federal and state clean water laws, one fifth of all animal and plant species cling to the edge of extinction, fisheries have collapsed, and deforestation has resulted in the removal of more than 90 percent of America's original forests. In July of 2011, the United Nations called global warming, biodiversity loss, and disturbance of the nitrogen-cycle balance *"a major planetary catastrophe."*

In fact, by almost all major environmental statistics, the health of the planet and our communities is worse now than before the creation of the federal Environmental Protection Agency and the adoption of the country's first major environmental laws over forty years ago.

Coming in the wake of *Silent Spring*, those laws, including the Clean Air Act and the Clean Water Act, were lauded as pioneering a new era of environmental protection. Similarly, the adoption of seminal labor laws in the 1930s was praised as creating a new era of protection for U.S. workers. The 1935 National Labor Relations Act was hailed as the "Magna Carta for workers." Yet, decades later, it is harder for workers to organize in the workplace, and the number of unionized workers has fallen precipitously while real wages have declined steadily over the past thirty years. And matters are getting worse. In recent years, many state legislatures have adopted laws that have stripped public and other employees of core labor rights, including the right to collectively bargain.[1]

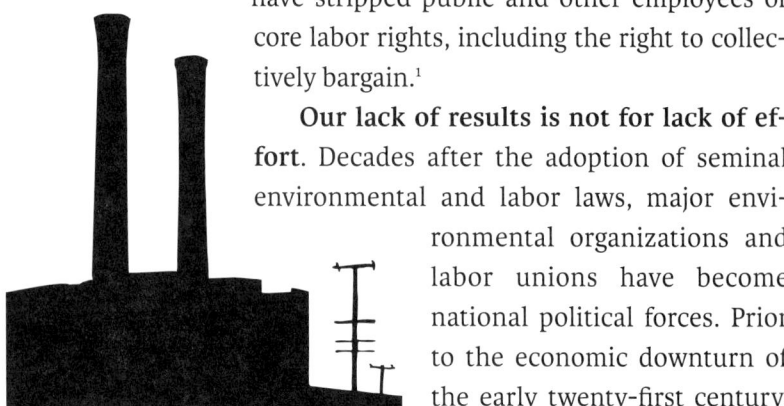

Our lack of results is not for lack of effort. Decades after the adoption of seminal environmental and labor laws, major environmental organizations and labor unions have become national political forces. Prior to the economic downturn of the early twenty-first century, labor spending on elections had been steadily increasing since the 1970s. Environmental groups raise and spend more than a billion dollars annually.

All of this would lead any objective observer to ask "Why?" Why, by almost every statistic, is the natural environment in worse shape now than prior to the adoption of those national environmental laws? And why, by almost every labor statistic, are workers in worse shape now than when those seminal labor laws were enacted?

WHY ENVIRONMENTAL AND LABOR LAWS DON'T WORK

A surprising notion to some, but certainly not to those who actually crafted those laws, **environmental and labor laws were *never intended to protect the rights of workers or the natural environment*.** Instead, in the case of workers, the major labor laws were adopted by Congress to protect commerce and stabilize the national economy by insulating them from labor "unrest" in the form of sit-downs, plant seizures, and strikes.[2] Similarly, major environmental laws were not adopted to protect the natural environment in and of itself, but to provide for the *orderly use* of the natural environment by industry and for other human wants and needs.[3]

Thus, labor laws were adopted to ensure an uninterrupted full-production economy, rather than protecting the rights of workers, and environmental laws were adopted to protect people's right to *use* natural resources in ways that would not adversely affect other people or property, rather than to protect the rights of nature or ecosystems. In many ways, the effect of those laws in protecting the rights of nature or workers is purely collateral, and occurs only when protection of those rights is necessary to ensure either a full-production economy or the orderly exploitation of natural resources.

Underpinning those goals was the explicit recognition by Congress that its authority for the adoption of those laws was conferred by the U.S. Constitution's Interstate Commerce Clause, which recognizes congressional authority to "regulate commerce . . . among the several states."[4] **Proponents of civil rights laws, environmental laws, and labor laws have long relied on the Commerce Clause to provide for congressional authority to adopt those laws.**[5]

The legality of civil rights laws thus was premised on African-Americans traveling between states as articles of commerce. Environmental laws were premised on waterways, birds, air, and waste as part of the stream of interstate commerce.[6] And labor laws were focused on the impact of labor unrest on the nation's commerce.[7]

Many respond to that critique by pointing out that the Constitution does not provide any other footing for Congress to act in these areas and that without the use of the Commerce Clause as congressional authority, those laws would never have been passed and upheld by the courts. That argument, however, carries the seed of its own repudiation—**an implicit recognition that the existing constitutional structure is not rights-based but commerce-based, which then requires an exploration of** *whether a structure solely focused on protecting commerce can ever provide a foundation for rights and sustainability*. Engaging in that inquiry requires examining whether a system constructed to protect the rights of those engaged in commercial activities (which is how the constitutional structure protects commerce) can serve to protect the rights of people and nature that inevitably run counter to the rights of those major commercial actors.

It is here that culture and law intersect. The U.S. Constitution provides a willing platform for lawmaking that protects and accelerates *"the production of endless more"*[8] precisely because that was one of the original intents of the constitutional structure—to accelerate the development of "endless" natural resources as a means of transforming the U.S. into a major international power. Laws impeding that expansion—such as "rights" laws that "interfere" with expansion and production in the name of protecting environmental and labor rights—are suppressed by the existing constitutional structure with outright hostility.

To withstand legal challenges to those laws, proponents have been forced to argue that the real focus of those laws was the facilitation of commerce, and thus that Congress possessed the authority under the Commerce Clause to pass them in the first place. That contortion—attempting to fit what would otherwise be "rights" laws into the box of commerce—then served to limit the political discussion around those laws. **Advocates for these laws began talking in terms of** *the benefit of environmental and labor laws to commerce,* **rather than their innate values that deserved protection on their own.** That, in turn, then programmed the next generation of advocates to work within that same box, which eventually produced a culture in which the natural environment and labor are only valued in terms of their contributions to commerce and the economy.

Thus, use of Congress's commerce power as the means to attempt to protect and secure rights comes at a great cost. It forces the transformation of rights laws into commercial and economic ones, and it frames the enforcement of those laws—as well as the debate and discussion surrounding them—on the commercial value of those protections.

The commercial success of the U.S. has reinforced that hamster wheel, along with the engorgement of a super-class of corporations. That, in turn, has enabled a corporate minority to create and nurture a "corporate culture"—a culture in which liberty, freedom, and progress cannot be achieved without a system tethered to the production of endless more.

HOW CERTAIN LEGAL DOCTRINES FURTHER RESTRICT ENVIRONMENTAL AND LABOR LAWS

In addition to the constitutional screen established by the Commerce Clause, three other areas of law have built walls around the enforcement of environmental and labor laws.

The first is the *legal treatment of nature and ecosystems as property*. Under law, ownership of property carries with it the right to destroy the ecosystems that exist on the property, and thus the right of the property owner automatically supersedes any inherent right claimed on behalf of the ecosystem.[9] In fact, because nature is not recognized as having any rights of its own, no contest of rights ever occurs—the only rights *seen* by the system of law are the rights of the property owner.

The second area of constitutional law that circumscribes the reach of these laws is the well-settled doctrine that *the property rights of business owners override the rights of workers in the workplace*.[10] The structure thus removes Bill of Rights constitutional protections from workers when they set foot over the threshold of workplaces owned by their private employers—withdrawing free speech, unreasonable search and seizure, equal protection, and due process rights from employees.

The third area of constitutional law that limits the application of environmental and labor laws is the *doctrine of corporate constitutional "rights."* Under that doctrine, corporations have been accorded First Amendment free speech protections, Fourth Amendment protections against warrantless searches, and Fifth Amendment guarantees of due process. They are further protected by prohibitions against the taking of property without compensation, and Fourteenth Amendment guarantees of due process and equal protection.

The history of corporate interests gaining constitutional protections—protections originally intended to shield natural persons from their own government—has its origins in our earliest days as a nation. The U.S. Supreme Court first recognized constitutional rights for certain corporations as early as 1819.[11] In 1886, in the infamous *Santa Clara* case, the Supreme Court declared that corporations were "persons" for purposes of parts of the Fourteenth Amendment to the Constitution.[12] This initiated a series of decisions that have bestowed most Bill of Rights protections upon corporations and, by extension, upon decision-makers who control those corporations. The *Citizens United* decision, while considered by many to be a unique and devastating blow to democracy, merely represented another application of constitutional powers previously bestowed on the corporate form.[13]

Because this nation's environmental and labor laws are limited by those constitutional provisions, while being codified under congressional authority to regulate interstate commerce, the reality on the ground falls short of the dreams and aspirations of those who politically drove the creation of those laws. *Because those laws began in the wrong frame, they are enforced within the wrong frame, and the public debate about them is set within the wrong frame.* In short, we continue to adopt, enforce, and debate those laws based on a misunderstanding of the constitutional context in which they were forged and are currently used.

Proceeding toward solutions premised on the correct frame of historical understanding means figuring out why the wrong template—one based on commerce and property rather than on the protection of rights—has been the default over the last century. Replacing that default is the key to restoring democratic decision-making that enables us to attain economic and environmental sustainability.

TWO

Why and How the U.S. Constitution Protects Property and Commerce

The roots of the federal Constitution lie in English common law—a system of law that developed after William the Conqueror's invasion of England in 1066. Using a system of judicial precedent characterized by the protection of property as the primary means of securing the rights of property owners, that structure of law was then perfected to authorize, defend, and protect colonialism as a means to expand the English empire.

Consequently, early English charters were used to replicate that system of law in the American colonies—elevating the rights of property and commerce over the rights of nature, communities, and majorities of indigenous peoples—by requiring that those Englishmen receiving colonial charters (packaged with large tracts of land, along with complete legislative, judicial, and executive powers of governance) adopt only those laws consistent with English law.[14]

Those who drafted the U.S. Constitution, while viewing the hereditary English Parliament with disdain, nevertheless viewed the English system of law as the world's most advanced.[15] Based on the belief that a strong, decisive, and centralized federal government was necessary to place the country on a firm commercial setting (and that this was necessary for the defense and growth of the country, its power relative to other nations, and its prosperity), **the Constitution not only transformed the federal government into the supreme lawmaker of the land, but explicitly reserved to the** federal government the sole power to control and regulate commerce across the states.[16]

Seeing an almost unlimited supply of natural resources stretching across the horizon, the founders drafted a document protecting the rights of those who would turn those resources into products to be created, consumed, and exported. Such was the English model—*using state power to support the rights of colonizing corporations by protecting the rights of corporate decision-makers to do so.*

Protecting the rights of those engaged in that production necessarily required a limitation on the democratic rights of people who might otherwise interfere with that production. James Madison, the principal architect of the Constitution, stated it most clearly, explaining that in creating this new structure of law and governance, the purpose of the drafters was *"to protect the minority of the opulent against the majority."*[17]

That federal constitutional blueprint then set the stage for the development of other legal doctrines consistent with its underlying philosophy. Those doctrines include the doctrine of *corporate constitutional "rights,"* through which the federal courts bestowed the rights of persons onto corporations, enabling corporations to use those protections to overturn local and state laws.[18] *That legal development was a natural and logical one,* given that corporations were rapidly becoming the primary vehicles for constitutionally protected commerce. *Clothing their activities in the highest constitutional protections was intended to shield those entities from local and state control,* thus ensuring the ability of those actors to fulfill their role in commerce under the central constitutional theme.

The Constitution was drafted with an explicit clause rendering federal law supreme over state law,[19] **and over time, judicially expanded federal preemption was extended to eliminate almost all conflicting local and state lawmaking.** Thus, federal preemption was interpreted not only to prevent the enforcement of laws that interfered with existing federal law but also to prevent the adoption of laws that *might interfere* with federal lawmaking at some point in the future.[20]

In the same vein, the constitutional structure was interpreted to limit municipal lawmaking only to those areas explicitly granted to them by state governments, thus *denying a general right to self-government in every municipal community.*[21] Given the primary theme of centralization of decision-making authority over issues related to commerce and property, these doctrines emerged as logical prerequisites for the success of the federal constitutional blueprint in attaining the goals of its authors.[22]

Those doctrines have placed *a minority of state and federal decision-makers in positions to supersede laws adopted by community majorities.* Typically, state and federal legislators use preemption clauses within state and federal legislation to do so, which then become privately enforceable by corporations bringing suit against communities to enforce those preemption clauses. In that way, state power is harnessed by affected corporations through litigation in both state and federal courts.

Concurrent with that preemption of community decision-making, those benefiting from the existing system have also used those doctrines to insulate state and federal levels of government from democratic control. Wielding constitutional free speech rights, for example, corporations dominate political debate and discussion and, under the *Citizens United* case, now can use unlimited amounts of money to influence federal campaigns for election.[23]

DISGUISING COMMERCIAL PROTECTIONS AS DEMOCRACY

Unlike commerce and property, ecosystems and workers are not mentioned within the federal Constitution. The only mention of *labor* in the document refers to escaped slaves—mandating return of those slaves to the owners of that property. While the subordination of the rights of nature, communities, and workers to the interests of property and commerce may have made internal sense within the contours of the eighteenth century—to those framers building a governing system with property protection at its core—it has proven to be a less-than-viable framework for transitioning toward a society desperately seeking sustainability for its own survival.

As the old saying goes, fish discover water last. Backed by enormous, generations-old structures of wealth and accumulated power, those who benefit from the current structure of law have carefully camouflaged the workings of the system, so that people and communities are unable to fully grasp how it completely disempowers them. Enormous resources have been invested in policy think-tanks, the political parties, and advertising to shape how Americans view the system of government in which they live. Equating the current system of governance with the American "way of life," progress, and freedom, those benefiting from the current system have virtually made it impossible for anyone to believe that other systems could exist.

That *corporate culture* prevents people from seeing how they are harnessed to a system of law and production that prevents the creation of sustainable communities while virtually guaranteeing the destruction of the natural environment.[24]

Building a movement that fundamentally changes the structure of the current system requires that enough people penetrate the camouflage and fully understand how the current system operates, and who benefits from it. It then requires action that leverages that understanding at the grassroots level—action that poses a real and credible threat to the current structure, and that eventually transforms the structure by eradicating the old one.

It means *building the groundwork for a future uprising that will replace the current, property-based system of today with a system premised on sustainability.* Such a journey will require a massive effort to reveal to large numbers of people how the current system actually functions, and assisting those people within their own communities to envision and adopt a different system.

The challenge, then, is a complex one: *first*, how to assist communities and activists to understand how the structure of law actually operates and what cultural values it perpetuates; *second*, how to build a mass movement from those communities and activists to create new structures of law that elevate the rights of people, communities, and nature above competing commercial and property rights; and *third*, how to assist the movement to leverage those new structures of law to change state and federal constitutional structures—all the while under constant siege by the system's current beneficiaries, who will use the courts, legislatures, and other governmental and private mechanisms to stop the movement from building.

THREE

Energizing and Accelerating Necessary Constitutional Change

Changing the DNA of how the system currently operates means changing the Constitution to subordinate rights and protections for property and commerce, to the rights of people, communities, and nature.

Necessary federal constitutional change may be accomplished by a constitutional amendment, or it may require the writing of a new federal constitution. Which option must be pursued will be determined by which one would: a) create enough structural change to enable communities to use their lawmaking authority to create economic and environmental sustainability, and b) shield that assertion of lawmaking authority from nullification by corporate minorities asserting both corporate "rights" and state and federal preemptive legal frameworks.

The historical failure of constitutional amendments or other proposed constitutional changes to become law serves as a grim reminder of how difficult it is to drive changes to the federal Constitution. Successful movements like the Abolitionists and the Suffragists invested in widescale, national grassroots efforts that altered the national psyche, while harnessing that new mindset toward systemic and structural changes to the federal Constitution. Those cultural shifts were accompanied by numerous acts of disobedience, ranging from women invading voting booths to vote, to juries refusing to convict runaway slaves under fugitive slave laws mandating their return, to a range of slave revolts and violence. **Disobedience to existing law was the hallmark of those movements, and breaking existing laws** served both to reveal the unjust nature of those laws and to portray what a new system of law would look like.[25]

It is a sobering fact that Abolitionist efforts—from the earliest student efforts at Lane Seminary in Cincinnati, Ohio, to the eventual adoption of the Thirteenth, Fourteenth, and Fifteenth Amendments to the federal Constitution—required close to forty years and a full-blown civil insurrection to secure equal rights for African-Americans (in text, at least); and that the movement to secure voting rights for women required seventy years following the Seneca Falls, New York, convention and more than 450 state legislative campaigns pushing for suffrage amendments, while subsequently falling short of mandating equal rights across the board. While the difficulty of amending the Constitution often is referred to as proof of the brilliance of the founders (usually by those beneficiaries of the failure of those amendments), it has in fact served as the major obstacle to the recognition and expansion of human rights over the past two hundred years.

KEY LESSONS FROM PAST PEOPLE'S MOVEMENTS

Key lessons emerged from past people's movements—particularly from the Abolitionists and Suffragist movements—which must be incorporated into any movement for structural, constitutional change.

First, movements start not only small but local—and they begin with people who are personally impacted by a harm legalized by the existing constitutional structure. They begin with conversations among people with shared belief systems and then broaden to an ever-widening group. These discussions are all part of building a base of support for fundamental change and identifying people with the passion and capability to leverage those conversations to engage a more geographically and philosophically diverse population. The strategy, then, is to build more and more pockets of people, communities, and groups who support structural change and are willing to engage in an effort to make that change happen. As more and more pockets are engaged, the task remains to bring them together to form a larger movement working to drive change upward from the local level to the state and federal levels.[26]

The second key lesson of these past movements is that they started slowly and took significant time to build. Fundamental structural change comes neither easily nor quickly. In our culture of immediacy, advocates are considered to have failed if their work doesn't generate headlines today or thousands of Facebook fans. Thus, advocacy—and organizations that fund advocacy—are tailored to generate the immediate headlines and create the online storm of e-mails, blogs, and web postings that suggest that *something is happening*. But a listserv does not a movement make. And headlines are only as good as they are able to advance the organizing on the ground. By themselves, they have no value. Our expectation of instant results is cultural and is one we must counteract with a different story. It is partly a function of advertising leading people to expect  an instant fix for what ails them, and partly a result of not knowing the history and nature of movements.

A third key lesson is that these movements are characterized by traditional *failures*. For example, in the early years of the Abolitionist movement, anti-slavery organizations in Ohio, Massachusetts, Vermont, and elsewhere gathered thousands of signatures on petitions, which were then sent to Congress. For years, the House and Senate—led by their southern members—deliberately ignored the petitions by voting to table or outright reject them, rather than give them consideration or a hearing. Often, the petitions asked Congress to outlaw slavery in the District of Columbia. They failed time and time again. In the face of a strong and angry opposition, however, the Abolitionists were able to slowly build their movement by using the actions and words of slavery's defenders to bring more people into their fold.

For more than a century, Suffragists in the U.S. similarly struggled and suffered in their efforts to gain rights for women, including the right to vote. In the 1870s, following ratification of the Fourteenth Amendment, which recognized rights for newly freed slaves, Suffragists attempted to use the new amendment to force a recognition of universal suffrage. The courts uniformly rejected their efforts, yet the Suffragists attempted to vote in several elections and were arrested. Thwarted by the judiciary, the Suffragists were able to *use these failures* to strengthen and deepen their movement—understanding that with each so-called failure, they were shining an increasingly brighter light on the injustice and illegitimacy of laws denying women's rights—thus adding fuel to a movement that remained a constant between confrontations.

Core Abolitionists and Suffragists understood that contemporary institutions would seek to prevent their movements from building, and that those losses were inevitable by-products of building a movement. They understood that they had to find a way to use losses not as ends in themselves but as a means to attain long-term structural change that would ameliorate those short-term losses. Thus, failures are an inevitable and necessary part of waking up both activists and a wider public to the reality of the existing system.

A fourth lesson from these movements is that overturning legal doctrines that support current injustice requires frontal and direct breaking of existing laws. If unjust laws are not broken, they have the appearance of being valid because—in a self-fulfilling prophecy of their own—no one feels the necessity to violate them. Breaking those laws then creates a cognitive dissonance—between a future in which new doctrines are created versus a future in which those doctrines continue to reinforce unjust structures of power and treatment.

During the Civil Rights movement, this meant that four African-American college freshmen—Ezell Blair, Franklin McCain, Joseph McNeil, and David Richmond—would sit-in at the Woolworth counter in Greensboro, North Carolina. In doing so, they began to frame the segregation of lunch counters—as a cultural norm reinforced by law—as unjust. Although they did it because they believed segregation was a moral and ethical wrong, they soon became the spark for additional people to join—the four became twenty, the twenty became sixty, and the sixty quickly became three hundred. *The act to define the doctrine as unjust is the first step*; if it resonates with enough people in a similar plight, it has the potential to become a movement.

The Suffragists and Abolitionists followed similar trajectories—*staking their claims through clear, concise, and succinct distinctions between "just" and "unjust" laws.* Suffragists broke the law by casting ballots on election day.[27] Abolitionists broke laws banning the mailing of their literature into the South, by the refusal of Abolitionist juries to enforce the Fugitive Slave Act, and by calling into question the very legality of the U.S. Constitution.[28] The Civil Rights movement of the 1960s was equally replete with examples of law-breaking, including the violation of judicial injunctions aimed at stopping marches in Memphis and other cities.[29]

A fifth lesson from these movements is that, when people advocate for fundamental change—advocating for rights for those without them—they are described as treasonous and radical, their ideas are ridiculed, and even those who sympathize with their cause argue that the changes they seek are too big and come too fast. As part of the early Abolitionist movement at Lane Seminary, Ted Weld and his students were forcibly ejected from the seminary for their views. Indeed, the Abolitionists and Suffragists faced ridicule and were shunned by their families and society at large for the ideas they expressed.

As law professor Christopher Stone, author of the seminal work "Should Trees Have Standing?"[30] has explained:

> The fact is, that each time there is a movement to confer rights onto some new "entity" the proposal is bound to sound odd or frightening or laughable. This is partly because until the rightless thing receives its rights, we cannot see it as anything but a thing for the use of "us"—us being, of course, those of us who hold rights.

It is a formidable challenge to envision the building of a movement that—rather than working toward enfranchisement and liberty of certain classes of the population (requiring an extended, enormous amount of energy, resources, and belief, as revealed by the Abolitionists and Suffragists)—instead seeks to displace a centralized decision-making system focused on protecting property and commerce, with one that elevates the rights of people, communities, and nature above the rights of property and commerce. It is even more daunting to imagine a structure of law that elevates those rights as part of a movement aimed at securing environmental and economic sustainability.

That is, however, exactly what close to two hundred communities in Pennsylvania, Virginia, New Hampshire, Maryland, New York, Massachusetts, Ohio, New Mexico, Maine, Washington, Oregon, and California have begun to do with the assistance of the Community Environmental Legal Defense Fund (CELDF).

PUTTING IT ON THE GROUND: CODIFYING A NEW SYSTEM OF LAW

Beginning in 1999, rural Pennsylvania communities confronted corporate hog factory farms in their communities by banning agribusiness corporations from their municipalities. Those laws then evolved into laws banning corporate sludge dumping, longwall coal mining, large-scale water withdrawals, and unsustainable land development. They then further evolved to recognize communities' right to local self-government by eliminating competing claims to corporate "rights" of personhood, recognizing the rights of nature and ecosystems, and challenging the use of preemption to override local lawmaking.

The final transformation of those laws has involved using "community rights" frameworks to define sustainable farming, sustainable land development, and sustainable energy production within those municipalities. Those laws establish local bills of rights for communities, ecosystems, and residents, and then prohibit unsustainable practices that would violate those rights.[31] They protect those rights frameworks by redefining corporate rights and powers in those communities, and by limiting other legal doctrines routinely used to overturn municipal lawmaking.

In short, they have created a structure of rights and prohibitions which, when enforced, will define economic and environmental sustainability within their communities. Ultimately, these "sustainability laws" recognize that *sustainability is impossible unless we begin to remove those corporate legal doctrines that prevent communities from banning unsustainable activities within their municipalities.*

In essence, those municipal laws challenge the existing constitutional structure by creating an entirely new one. They then dare the corporate beneficiaries of the existing structure to challenge those laws and, in the process, harness corporate resources to remove the camouflage about how the system currently functions. By being forced to leverage corporate resources and publicly illustrating (in real time) how the existing structure nullifies community lawmaking, more and more people arrive at the realization that the structure is inherently unjust and undemocratic.

As part of a self-enhancing cycle, the corporate challenge (and resulting judicial decision) thus clarifies for a broader segment of the public how the constitutional structure operates and why it must be changed. The process also allows lawyers for the communities to lay out and explain to judges and courts why a new structure of law is necessary, and how that new structure of law could operate.

Communities working to create new structures of law did not begin their journey with a historical examination of the failure of this country's environmental and labor laws. They were sparked, usually, by a single corporation threatening their community with a specific project followed by the community's attempt to seek refuge under existing laws. Subsequently, the people of those communities discovered that those *environmental laws did not protect them from the project, and that the community lacked the legal authority to stop the corporation from harming them.*[32] It is precisely that awakening that compelled them to learn how the structure of law subordinated them to both corporations and preemptive state and federal governments, and then take action to reject the existing structure and create another.

As is expected, these assertions of local self-governance within a structure that systematically deprives communities of self-determination (especially when that self-determination runs counter to existing constitutional protections for property and commerce) have been met by lawsuits from corporations affected by the local lawmaking. Those lawsuits seek to overturn those local laws using preemptive state and federal regulatory frameworks and to punish those localities by seeking monetary judgments for the violation of the corporation's "rights."

ORGANIZING JUJITSU: TURNING THE RESOURCES OF THE AGGRESSOR AGAINST ITSELF

Applying key lessons from prior movements means that we must make organizing platforms out of those lawsuits—treating them not as distractions, but as *opportunities*, in much the same way as the Abolitionists and Suffragists viewed opposition to their efforts.

That means frontally challenging long-settled legal doctrines as denials of the right to community self-government, and using eventual rulings as *proofs* of how the structure actually operates.

People then must leverage those proofs to drive more and more people toward more and more confrontations between their communities and the structure of law.

Much like using single matches to illuminate a painting in a dark room, enough matches need to be struck simultaneously (and burn long enough) so that the painting can be viewed in its entirety. Each municipality is a match, and each instance of a law being overturned as violative of these legal doctrines is an opportunity for people to see how the structure actually functions.[33] This does the necessary work of penetrating the denial, piercing the illusion of democracy, and removing the blinders that prevent a large majority of people from seeing the reality on the ground.

Being able to see what is so, and to contrast this reality with our myths and our values of equality and fairness under the law, will eventually foment cultural change. If those confrontations are numerous enough, a growing understanding by more and more people will create a movement focused on fundamentally overhauling the existing constitutional structure to bring it into alignment with that cultural shift.

In this organizing process, local laws are no longer merely local laws. They become nascent constitution-making in that the local laws begin to resemble *municipal constitutions* that codify a new structure of law.

Eventually, thousands of municipal constitutions will emerge and, just as the Declaration of Independence was constructed from other declarations adopted by municipal jurisdictions,[34] **local constitutions will provide a template for new state and federal constitutional structures.**[35] Those new constitutions will contain several common denominators that transcend all single-issue areas: expanding rights for people, communities, and nature by eliminating certain types of state and federal preemption; removing corporate "rights" that conflict with rights recognized by the municipality; and elevating nature and ecosystems from the status of mere property to that of rights-bearing entities.

FOUR

Driving the Local into the State

Building a national movement based on community disobedience to the existing structure of law requires a continuous stream of people within communities focused on structural change. Without that continuous stream, communities working toward municipal lawmaking will not produce a strong enough united front necessary to force changes to state and federal constitutions.

To be relevant around a variety of issues, replication must occur by issue area and by geographic proximity. As an example, CELDF drafted a Sustainable Food Systems Ordinance for the residents of several municipalities, which is now being used by groups working on sustainable food issues across the country.[36] Thus, the ordinance became a means of transforming the work of issue-focused groups toward advancing a rights-based framework of organizing. Similarly, after the first CELDF-drafted corporate farming ordinance was adopted in Wells Township in Fulton County, Pennsylvania, it was then replicated in other municipalities across Fulton County, and then in municipalities across that region of the state.

Creating state constitutional change requires large segments of the population of a state advocating for that change. This organizing must therefore be done in both rural and urban communities, and must find relevancy to issues in large cities as well as small municipalities.

In 2007, CELDF began working in Spokane, Washington, assisting in the creation of Envision Spokane, a coalition of twenty-four labor union locals, community nonprofit organizations, and neighborhood associations, to place a Community Bill of Rights onto the 2009 election ballot as a citizens' initiative. The Bill of Rights sought to decentralize decision-making power over certain development projects, while recognizing rights to affordable housing, preventive healthcare, and rights in the workplace. Lacking a single cohesive issue or assault, the work in Spokane was focused purely on constructing a rights framework that would enable neighborhood, labor, and other organizations to achieve goals that had been previously unattainable due to structural constraints. Although the measure failed to pass in 2009, the coalition qualified a shorter version in 2011, which narrowly missed adoption by a swing of only five hundred votes.[37]

In November of 2010, the City of Pittsburgh became the first major metropolitan area to adopt a CELDF-drafted ordinance. Created to confront natural gas drilling proposed within the city, the ordinance contains a bill of rights for city residents, recognizes the rights of nature, and challenges corporate-claimed constitutional "rights" within the municipality. In alignment with other municipalities, the central theme of the city's ordinance is to recognize expanded civil rights and then secure those rights by prohibiting activities, such as commercial gas extraction, that would violate those rights.

At the time of this writing, **close to two hundred municipalities in ten states have adopted similar laws**, backed by citizen organizing that seeks not only to adopt local laws but also to enforce them.

FOMENTING STATE CONSTITUTIONAL CHANGE THROUGH COLLECTIVE MUNICIPAL LEGISLATIVE CIVIL DISOBEDIENCE

Once a critical mass of municipalities within each state adopts laws that feature common lawmaking elements, those municipalities must then stitch themselves together to begin moving toward state constitutional change that will protect those local laws while *constitutionalizing* the common elements of them.

In early 2010, in Pennsylvania—the first state in which a critical mass of municipalities emerged that are engaged in this new lawmaking—municipal representatives gathered to discuss collectively codifying those legal frameworks into their state constitutions. The initial result of that collaboration was the approval of the "Chambersburg Declaration" and the establishment of a statewide organization—the Pennsylvania Community Rights Network (PACRN).

The Declaration of the PACRN reads:

THE CHAMBERSBURG DECLARATION
By the Undersigned in Chambersburg, Pennsylvania, on Saturday, February 20th, 2010

We declare:

- That the political, legal, and economic systems of the United States allow, in each generation, an elite few to impose policy and governing decisions that threaten the very survival of human and natural communities;
- That the goal of those decisions is to concentrate wealth and greater governing power through the exploitation of human and natural communities, while promoting the belief that such exploitation is necessary for the common good;
- That the survival of our communities depends on replacing this system of governance by the privileged with new community-based democratic decision-making systems;
- That environmental and economic sustainability can be achieved only when the people affected by governing decisions are the ones who make them;
- That, for the past two centuries, people have been unable to secure economic and environmental sustainability primarily

through the existing minority-rule system, laboring under the myth that we live in a democracy;
- That most reformers and activists have not focused on replacing the current system of elite decision-making with a democratic one, but have concentrated merely on lobbying the factions in power to make better decisions; and
- That reformers and activists have not halted the destruction of our human or natural communities because they have viewed economic and environmental ills as isolated problems, rather than as symptoms produced by the absence of democracy.

Therefore, let it be resolved:

- That a people's movement must be created with a goal of revoking the authority of the corporate minority to impose political, legal, and economic systems that endanger our human and natural communities;
- That such a movement shall begin in the municipal communities of Pennsylvania;
- That we, the people, must transform our individual community struggles into new frameworks of law that dismantle the existing undemocratic systems while codifying new, sustainable systems;
- That such a movement must grow and accelerate through the work of people in all municipalities to raise the profile of this work at state and national levels;
- That when corporate and governmental decision-makers challenge the people's right to assert local, community self-governance through passage of municipal law, the people, through their municipal governments, must openly and frontally defy those legal and political doctrines that subordinate the rights of the people to the privileges of a few;
- That those doctrines include preemption, subordination of municipal governments, bestowal of constitutional rights

upon corporations, and relegating ecosystems to the status of property;
- That those communities in defiance of rights-denying law must join with other communities in our state and across the nation to envision and build new state and federal constitutional structures that codify new, rights-asserting systems of governance;
- That Pennsylvania communities have worked for more than a decade to advance those new systems and, therefore, have the responsibility to become the first communities to call for a new state constitutional structure; and
- That now, this 20th day of February, 2010, the undersigned pledge to begin that work, which will drive the right to local, community self-government into the Pennsylvania Constitution, thus liberating Pennsylvania communities from the legal and political doctrines that prevent them from building economically and environmentally sustainable communities.

That a Call Issues from this Gathering:

- To create a network of people committed to securing the right to local, community self-government, the reversal of political, legal, and cultural doctrines that interfere with that right, and the creation of a new system and doctrines that support that right;
- To call upon the people and elected officials across the Commonwealth of Pennsylvania to convene a larger gathering of delegates representing their municipal communities, who will propose constitutional changes to secure the right of local, community self-government; and
- To create the people's movement that will result in these changes to the Pennsylvania Constitution.

In 2012, communities in New Mexico and Washington State gathered to produce their own declarations. In New Mexico, the communities created the New Mexico Coalition for Community Rights, and in Washington State, the communities created the Washington Community Rights Network. The New Mexico Declaration reads:

THE MORA COUNTY [NEW MEXICO] DECLARATION

We, the undersigned residents of New Mexico and the communities in which we live, hereby declare the following:

Whereas, our communities are under siege from oil and gas, agribusiness, energy, and other corporations;

Whereas, our communities are under siege from a structure of law that has bestowed greater rights on those corporations than the communities in which they operate, and it is that system of law that enables the corporations to do what they do;

Whereas, we recognize that such a system grants a corporate minority the legal authority to override our community majorities;

Whereas, we recognize that economic and environmental sustainability have been rendered illegal under this system of law, and that this system is not democratic;

Whereas, given the control by those corporations over our elected representatives, we have given up hope that either our state government or the federal government will help protect us from these corporations;

Whereas, we declare that if democracy means "majority rule" and "consent of the governed," that a democracy does not exist in our communities, or in the State of New Mexico, and that we must now create democracy in our municipalities and within the State; and

Whereas, we now call on communities across the State of New Mexico to do the following:

- Adopt local laws that recognize community rights for residents of New Mexico municipalities and the natural environment;
- Include in those local laws direct challenges to the legal doctrines that currently mandate that corporations have greater rights than residents of our communities;
- Join together with other communities across the State to create a statewide movement focused on rewriting the State Constitution to recognize a right to local self-government which eliminates these legal doctrines at the State level, to protect the local laws adopted within our municipalities; and
- Join together with other statewide movements to rewrite the federal Constitution to elevate the rights of people and communities above the claimed rights of corporations.

The Washington Community Rights Network Declaration reads:

THE SPOKANE DECLARATION

We, the residents of Washington State and of our communities, gathering in Spokane, Washington, this 28th day of July, 2012, declare:

Whereas, our communities are under siege from corporations exploiting our communities for resource extraction and a variety of other uses harmful to us and the natural environment;

Whereas, our communities are under siege from a structure of law that has bestowed greater rights on those corporations than the communities in which they operate;

Whereas, we recognize that such a system grants a corporate minority the legal authority to override our community majorities;

Whereas, we recognize that this system of law renders economic and environmental sustainability illegal and impossible;

Whereas, we have given up hope that our local, state, or federal government will protect us from these harms;

Therefore, we declare that if democracy means "consent of the governed," a democracy does not exist in our communities or in Washington State, and that we must now create democracy in our municipalities and within the State; and

We now call on communities across the State of Washington to:

- Adopt local laws that recognize community rights for residents of Washington municipalities and the natural environment;
- Include in those local laws direct challenges to the legal doctrines that currently mandate that corporations have greater rights than residents of our communities or the natural environment;
- Build a statewide coalition of communities to change the State Constitution to recognize our right to local self-government eliminating these legal doctrines at the State level, to protect the local laws adopted within our municipalities; and
- Join together with other statewide movements to change the federal Constitution to elevate the rights of people, communities, and nature above the claimed rights of corporations.

Those coalitions eventually may choose to work within the existing structure for constitutional change—New Hampshire, for example, places an automatic call for a constitutional convention on the ballot every ten years, or they may choose to convene a completely independent constitutional convention composed of representatives from towns and other municipalities joined by representatives of community and other nonprofit organizations. Other states provide for citizen-initiated constitutional changes, while others retain plenary control over constitutional changes within the state legislature.

Either way, for the state effort to support the local work, the unadulterated lawmaking efforts at the municipal level must be protected by—and then driven into—state constitutional structures.

Protecting the municipal lawmaking first means introducing and adopting state constitutional amendments that shield the municipal laws from corporate challenges and state preemption. In 2014, the Colorado Community Rights Network (COCRN) introduced a proposal to amend their state constitution with language that would insulate local bills of rights from both corporations and the state government. The proposal was immediately met with a legal challenge by the oil and gas industry, which sought to bar the proposal from the statewide ballot. The COCRN successfully fought the industry lawsuit, and obtained a ruling from the Colorado Supreme Court, which allowed the proposed measure to be circulated for signature and placed onto the statewide ballot. The measure, which is now being replicated by Networks in other states, reads:

Section 32. Right to Local Self-Government (new)
  (1) As all political power is vested in and derived from the people, and as all government of right originates from the people, the people have an inherent and inalienable right to local self-government, in each county, city, town, and other municipality.
  (2) That right shall include, without limitation:
      a. The power to enact local laws protecting health, safety, and welfare by establishing the fundamental rights of individuals, their communities, and nature, and by securing those rights using prohibitions and other means; and
      b. The power to enact local laws establishing, defining, altering, or eliminating the rights,

powers, and duties of corporations and other business entities operating or seeking to operate in the community, to prevent such rights and powers from interfering with such locally-enacted fundamental rights of individuals, their communities, and nature.
(3) Local laws adopted pursuant to subsection (2) of this section shall not be subject to preemption by international, federal, or state laws, nor shall they be subject to limitation pursuant to section 6 of article XX of this constitution; provided that:
    a. Such local laws shall not restrict fundamental rights of individuals, their communities, or nature secured by the Colorado constitution, the United States constitution, or international law; and
    b. Such local laws shall not weaken protections for individuals, their communities, or nature provided by state, federal, or international law.
(4) All provisions of this section are self-executing and severable.

This first round of constitutional change must be focused on *protecting* local lawmaking from predictable challenges by corporations and "higher" levels of government. The second round of constitutional change must seek to *drive the content and substance of the local enactments directly into state constitutions,* thus making state governments themselves the guarantor of the rights currently secured by the local enactments.

STATE CONSTITUTIONAL CHANGES: THE PROCESS AND WHAT THEY MAY LOOK LIKE

Each state has a different process for making constitutional change. In some, the people of the state can propose those changes, while in the vast majority of states control over constitutional amendments has been given exclusively to the state legislature. In those places, it is exceedingly unlikely that state legislatures will voluntarily place amendments to their constitutions onto the ballot, which would elevate community interests above the interests that currently fund, influence, and control the players and functioning of the legislatures themselves.

Accordingly, any rights-based movement will use the tools available for constitutional change in those states in which constitutional changes can be directly proposed, while creating new tools that can be used to force constitutional changes in those places in which the legislatures control the course of constitution-making. That may involve creating mechanisms for that change to occur directly through the people—generating a democratic, open process through which a popular referendum can be held, which then places increasing pressure on legislative systems to adopt those provisions.[38] Or, we may have arrived at a point whereby those independent, people-driven decision-making systems must directly supplant a legislative system more interested in enhancing state decision-making power than in building sustainability and recognizing the inherent, legitimate power of democratic majorities.

In Pennsylvania, power to place constitutional changes on the ballot rests entirely with the legislature under the current legal structure. Efforts have begun to draft a framework for what state constitutional changes may look like, using the common denominators that have emerged from the municipal laws adopted across the state. One such effort would require the amendment of the Pennsylvania Declaration of Rights with several new rights-frameworks which may appear as the following[39]:

Draft Amendments to the Pennsylvania Declaration of Rights

Section 29. People's Right to Local, Community Self-Government
The people of each municipality have an inherent and inalienable right to local, community self-government, which shall include the power to enact local laws protecting health, safety, and welfare by establishing the fundamental rights of individuals, their communities, and nature, and the power to secure those rights using prohibitions and other means. Those local laws shall not be preempted by state, federal, or international law if they do not restrict fundamental rights of individuals, their communities, or nature secured by the Pennsylvania constitution, the United States constitution, or international law; and if they do not weaken protections for individuals, their communities, or nature provided by state, federal, or international law.

Section 30. People's Rights Superior to Corporate Powers
Corporations and other business entities that violate rights secured by this Constitution shall not be "persons" under this Constitution or the laws of the Commonwealth, nor possess legal rights, privileges, powers, standing, or other protections that interfere with enforcement of rights secured by this Constitution or that interfere with the enforcement of local laws adopted pursuant to the people's right to local, community self-government.

Section 31. Rights of Nature
Natural communities and ecosystems within the Commonwealth possess inherent and inalienable rights to exist, persist, evolve, maintain themselves, and regenerate their own vital cycles, structure, functions, and processes. The Commonwealth, municipal governments, and each resident of the Commonwealth

shall possess standing to enforce these rights on behalf of natural communities and ecosystems.

Section 32. Right to Enforce Civil and Political Rights Against Private and Public Entities

The people of the Commonwealth of Pennsylvania possess the right to enforce their rights, as secured by this Constitution and by the exercise of the people's right to local, community self-government, against corporations, other business entities chartered by the Commonwealth or organized under the laws of the Commonwealth, and governmental entities.

Section 33. Property and Equal Governmental Participation

An enormous proportion of property vested in a few individuals is dangerous to rights, and destructive of the common happiness of humankind; and therefore every community and government has a right by its laws to discourage the possession of such property. Every person, regardless of wealth, shall be entitled to equal access to, participation in, and use of, all legislative and judicial organs of government. No person or group of persons shall have an advantage, by virtue of wealth, in elections, appointments, lawmaking, influence of public opinion, development of jurisprudence, or judicial contests, and both state and local governments shall have an affirmative duty to enforce these provisions through law and policy.

Section 34. Right of the People to Change the Constitution

The people of the Commonwealth possess the inalienable and indefeasible right to amend, alter, or abolish their current Constitution. A call for amending the Constitution made by ten percent of the electors of the Commonwealth shall require the Secretary of State to submit such amendments to the electorate at the next primary or general election, and approval of the amendments by a majority shall render the amendments effective. A call for a new Constitution made by twenty-five percent of the electors of the Commonwealth shall require the Secretary of State to design a non-partisan plan of representation for a new constitutional convention in which each borough, township, and town within the counties of the State, and each ward or equivalent unit within cities, receives direct and equal representation. The Secretary shall convene the convention no later than twelve months following the submission of the call, and the convention shall dissolve no later than twenty-four months after the call is made. A new proposed Constitution, if one has been adopted by a majority of the convention representatives, shall then be submitted to the electorate for a vote at the next primary or general election, and majority approval of the new Constitution shall render it effective. Amendments and new Constitutions shall never have the effect of contracting or diminishing the plain meaning and liberating intent of the Declaration of Rights, but shall only expand upon those rights and guarantee rights against infringement by all parties, public and private.

In states like Pennsylvania, communities must not only propose constitutional changes, but must also decide how to proceed with adopting those changes into law. Given the almost plenary control by the legislature over constitutional amendments (and no legislative process in Pennsylvania for a constitutional convention), the situation may give rise to an independent, community-called constitutional convention, which then demands that these changes be driven into the Pennsylvania Constitution. Taken to its logical conclusion, if such a demand is not recognized, communities could create their own ballot systems to adopt these constitutional changes into law, thus threatening the very legitimacy of the existing system.[40]

FIVE

Driving the Local and the State Upward into the National

As pressure grows from the local level, it will drive state constitutional change. As pressure grows from the coalitions of local communities working at the state level, those state frameworks eventually will force realignment of the federal constitutional structures. To prepare for that eventuality, the state Community Rights Networks created the **National Community Rights Network (NCRN)** in 2013. Its purpose is to serve as a national voice for the state-based community rights networks, with a board composed of representatives from those networks.

In October 2014, delegates from the state-based community rights networks gathered for the first time to discuss and propose federal constitutional changes necessary to eliminate federal legal hurdles to the expansion of sustainability rights at the local and state levels. As an organization, those delegates and others have begun a process of envisioning what federal constitutional change would look like, and how the organization can assist organizing in different states.

Aligning the federal constitutional structure to local and state rights-based lawmaking might consist of the following:

> (1) <u>A federal recognition of the right of local, community self-government</u>: Such a provision would provide a federal guarantee of the right of people within their own local communities to self-govern. That right to self-govern would include the adoption of laws which

enhance and expand civil, political, and environmental rights; and protection of those laws from the assertion of the doctrines of corporate "rights," preemption, and the subordinancy of municipal governments to other levels of government.

(2) Federal preemption: Such a provision would restrict federal preemption to the establishment of legislative and regulatory floors, rather than ceilings, for state and local lawmaking.

(3) Commerce Clause and Contracts Clause: Restriction of the Commerce Clause and Contracts Clause of the Constitution to recognize the authority of community lawmaking in the areas of commerce and contracts. This would either mean an elimination of those Clauses from the Constitution, or changes that would limit the reach of those Clauses.

(4) Corporate "rights": Elimination of constitutional and other legal "rights" for corporations, including corporate "personhood." This would mean an amendment to the Constitution which establishes that the Bill of Rights, and other amendments, are intended for the protection of natural persons only, and not for the protection of corporations or other business entities.

(5) Rights of nature: Recognizing and securing rights for nature and ecosystems. This would mean the creation of a "rights of nature" amendment to the Constitution that would provide for certain rights for natural communities and ecosystems, and for enforceability of those rights by governments, communities, and people.

(6) Expanding the Bill of Rights: Expansion of the rights of people to include additional civil, political, social, and economic rights as part of the Bill of Rights of the Constitution. This change would require the insertion

into the federal Constitution of some of the core "rights to sustainability" which are beginning to emerge at the community level.

Given the fact that the U.S. Constitution is essentially a property and commerce document, and that the changes to the document that must be made to ***transform it into a sustainability constitution*** are therefore of such great magnitude, a rewrite of the Constitution may be necessary.[41] Given that the document was originally drafted in the 1780s, the time for such a rewrite—that incorporates everything that we now know about ecosystems and planetary health—may have arrived.

SIX
An Invitation

This pamphlet serves as an invitation to action to community leaders, financial supporters of activism, and to environmental, labor, and other organizations working to secure and protect the rights of people, communities, workers, and nature.

For the change outlined by this pamphlet to come into being, activists must change the work that they do—from trying to make this system work for them to replacing that system with one that will. Funders must recognize the necessity of changing the structure, and organizations must change their modes of organizing, their campaigns, and their identities.

Currently, vast amounts of money and hours are expended daily by people seeking to *influence the operation* of our economic and legal systems, and to change our corporate culture. Most of that work, while sometimes preventing the worst from occurring, is likely to come to naught *without a focus on changing the structure itself.*

On the organizing front, municipalities and organizations must understand that this is a long-term strategy aimed at making fundamental structural change to the U.S. constitutional system.[42] This means that the adoption of an ordinance is merely a way-station toward combining with other communities to force that structural change at state and federal levels. It means that more and more community leaders and organizers must understand that this work requires a different type of commitment than conventional organizing, and that it requires those individuals to become catalysts of their own, taking the time to learn and understand the organizing strategy and then use their networks to bring more and more communities into the fold.

For traditional environmental and labor organizations, it means rethinking existing strategy, diverting resources away from their conventional organizing, and leveraging those resources to build creative campaigns that incorporate aspects of this work. It means engaging other environmental and labor organizations to convince the leadership of those groups to grapple with how the existing structure prevents their organizations from ever attaining the goals set forth by their respective memberships.

For funders, both individual and organizational, it means understanding that this work requires substantial investment geared toward long-term results. Multi-year funding for organizations engaged in this organizing, as well as a different sense of metrics to define success and failure, must be developed to accelerate and measure this work.

CELDF presents this pamphlet as an invitation to organizations and communities across the country to engage with us to find creative and effective approaches that collectively advance this work across a spectrum of issues, including those intimately affecting the environment, public health, labor, and social justice.

It is our hope that the massive amounts of time and resources currently invested in making the current system operate as humanely as possible can be diverted to the construction of a new system. *In the words of others, we can choose to be hospice workers to a dying planet—seeking to ease its transition—or we can choose to be midwives to a different system waiting to be born.*

That small choice, by each of us as individuals, may make all of the difference in the world.

Notes

1. In 2011, Wisconsin's legislature became the first of several state legislatures to legislatively remove the ability of public employees to collectively bargain over certain aspects of their employment.
2. The National Labor Relations Act (NLRA) begins by declaring that the intent of the law is to eliminate "strikes and other forms of industrial strife or unrest which have the intent or the necessary effect of burdening or obstructing commerce." See 29 U.S.C. §151. The Taft-Hartley Act of 1947 undermined workers' rights by allowing state legislatures to ban the union shop, made sympathy strikes and secondary boycotts illegal for all practical purposes, removed union control of pension funds and health and welfare funds, and enabled employers to actively and vocally oppose organizing. In several ways, that Act codified U.S. Supreme Court rulings that had eroded the protections of the NLRA, including the nullification of the requirement that employers remain neutral during unionizing campaigns.
3. This goal, of protecting the ability of people to exploit nature in an orderly and regulated way, is reflected by state constitutional environmental protection provisions adopted by several states. As an example, Article I, §27 of the Pennsylvania Constitution declares "natural resources" as "common property" to be used for the "benefit of all the people." While many environmental groups advocate for a model by which nature should be treated as "common property" or "the commons," such treatment does not change the status of ecosystems from being property (legally incapable of possessing rights) into independent systems with rights enforceable against certain activities that would violate those rights. Thus, as property subordinate to an "owner," current environmental protection efforts are almost purely focused on protecting those aspects of nature that are beneficial to people, rather than focusing on protecting the right of those natural systems to exist and flourish on their own.
4. The Interstate Commerce Clause can be found in Article I, §8, cl.3 of the U.S. Constitution. It is generally referred to as the "Commerce Clause."

5. One reason for Congress's almost total reliance on the Commerce Clause for this authority is because the U.S. Constitution elevates and protects property and commerce, but does not recognize nature or labor. In the text of the Constitution, interstate commerce was given the highest protections by the constitutional structure because of the value of commerce and production to an emerging nation. Later proponents of civil rights, environmental, and labor legislation sought to gird their legislation with the most powerful parts of the Constitution, logically using the Commerce Clause as the foundational authority for that legislation.
6. Thus arose doctrines like the "reasonable bird rule," used by the U.S. Supreme Court to determine whether certain wetlands are actually interstate, and thus under the authority of Congress and the Environmental Protection Agency through the federal Clean Water Act. The current test to determine whether certain wetlands are protected by the Clean Water Act is whether a "reasonable" migratory bird flying between states (as an article of commerce) would land on a particular waterway, and thus give jurisdiction to the EPA to enforce protections under the Clean Water Act for those wetlands.
7. As the National Labor Relations Act itself explains, ending those activities that "affect the flow of raw materials or manufactured or processed goods from or into the channels of commerce" or "disrupt the market for goods flowing from or into the channels of commerce" was the purpose of the law. The right to collectively organize, which was recognized by the law, thus was based on the preservation of commerce, not on workers' rights as a fundamental, non-economic value. See 29 U.S.C. §151.
8. A phrase originally conceived by historian Richard L. Grossman, it evokes a system of law whose primary reason for being is to support private market production by eliminating contrary laws that interfere with that production. The closest legal school of thought that mirrors this concept derives from the work of the University of Chicago Law School's Professor Richard Epstein, which posits that regulation of the marketplace is only appropriate when it serves to reinforce and enhance "naturally occurring" market forces.
9. Although briefly summarized here in two sentences, nature as property is an overriding theme of Western legal dogma. It is one explicitly rejected by indigenous cultures.
10. This doctrine, based on private property principles, virtually treats workers as guests on their employer's property, thus subjecting workers

to a lesser status than the owner of the property. This doctrine has been deemed to be so "well-settled" that challenges to it are rarely made even in academic circles.

11. *Trustees of Dartmouth College v. Woodward*, 17 U.S. (4 Wheat.) 518 (1819). In *Dartmouth*, the U.S. Supreme Court found that private corporations were entitled to protections under the Contracts Clause of the U.S. Constitution. Specifically, the Court declared that the charters of private corporations were "contracts" and thus could not be unilaterally altered by the state governments which had granted them.

12. *Santa Clara County v. Southern Pacific Railroad Company*, 118 U.S. 394 (1886).

13. *Citizens United v. Federal Election Commission*, 130 S.Ct. 876 (2010) (overturning congressional limitation of corporate electoral spending as a violation of corporate free speech "rights").

14. The charters were not subtle. The charter giving Pennsylvania to William Penn declared that the gift was made because of Penn's "commendable desire to enlarge our English Empire," and that all laws created by Penn must "bee [sic] not repugnant nor contrary" to English common law. See Penn Charter at preamble and section VI.

15. Not surprising, given that almost all lawbooks were English, many of the constitutional drafters were lawyers, and most were large property owners. Despite their political differences, they readily agreed that the best method to protect human rights (at least the rights of white property owners) was an English system of law that elevated the right to own and use property over other competing rights.

16. The Annapolis Convention, the forerunner of the Philadelphia Constitutional Convention, was focused almost entirely on the necessity of removing trade and commerce powers from individual states, and centralizing that power within a new, preemptive federal government. It was the report of the Annapolis Convention that created the call for the Philadelphia Constitutional Convention.

17. Hon. Robert Yates, *Notes of the Secret Debates of the Federal Convention of 1787, Taken by the Late Honorable Robert Yates, Chief Justice of the State of New York, and One of the Delegates from that State to the Said Convention*, entry of June 26, 1787.

18. See previous section. Corporate property, of course, was protected by the Commerce Clause long before corporations were recognized as persons, and corporations were wrapped in additional constitutional protections

by the Supreme Court in the *Dartmouth College* case of 1819. Although many observers point to the Supreme Court's 1886 *Santa Clara* decision as the seminal moment for corporate personhood, many legal commentators, including former Supreme Court Justice William J. Brennan, have traced the doctrine back to federal court decisions of the 1840s, and even further back to religious institutions of the previous century.

19. The "Supremacy Clause" of the U.S. Constitution declares, in Article VI, para. 2, that the federal constitution "shall be the supreme Law of the Land."

20. Known as the "dormant" Commerce Clause, the legal doctrine prevents municipalities and states from legislating in areas related to interstate commerce if the federal government may choose to legislate in that area sometime in the future.

21. Known as "Dillon's Rule" for its author, railroad lawyer John Forrest Dillon, the legal doctrine establishes a parent-child relationship between the states and municipal governments, with municipalities prohibited from passing laws unless those laws are specifically authorized by state legislatures.

22. As explained by James Madison, such was the original intent of some of the founders in subordinating state governments to the federal government. At the Philadelphia Convention, Madison exclaimed that "the States ought to be placed under the control of the general government—at least as much so as they formerly were under the king and British Parliament." Yates, *Notes of the Secret Debates*, entry of June 29, 1787.

23. *Citizens United v. Federal Election Commission*, 130 S.Ct. 876 (2010). Although cited as a seminal elections case, free speech "rights" claimed by corporations are nothing new. See, e.g., *First National Bank of Boston v. Bellotti*, 435 U.S. 765 (1978) (overturning a ban on corporate participation in referenda as being violative of free speech protections).

24. Indeed, that camouflage has been so successful that people routinely refer to the workings of the American system as a democracy.

25. In the words of Susan B. Anthony at her sentencing hearing (for casting a ballot in a presidential election), "Resistance to tyranny is obedience to God." *An Account of the Proceedings on the Trial of Susan B. Anthony on the Charge of Illegal Voting* 81–85 (1874).

26. The Suffragist movement offers an excellent example of this proposition. Starting with local Suffragist clubs in each state, those clubs then united to win the right to vote in several states, and the momentum from

victories in those states (mostly western ones) created the opportunity for the adoption of the Nineteenth Amendment, which was nationally ratified in 1920.

27. See, e.g., *An Account of the Proceedings on the Trial of Susan B. Anthony on the Charge of Illegal Voting* (1874).

28. See William Lloyd Garrison, "The United States Constitution," *Selections from the Writings and Speeches of William Lloyd Garrison* (1852), (noting that Garrison, on at least one occasion, burned a copy of the U.S. Constitution to make his point that the Constitution codified slavery and was thus illegitimate).

29. See Martin Luther King Jr., *I Have a Dream: Writings and Speeches That Changed the World* (New York: HarperCollins, 1992), 197.

30. Stone originally published a law review article titled "Should Trees Have Standing—Toward Legal Rights for Natural Objects," *Southern California Law Review* 45 (1972): 450–87, arguing that natural objects should have inherent rights of their own.

31. As an example of this lawmaking, in November 2010, the City Council of the City of Pittsburgh adopted an ordinance establishing a bill of rights that included the right to water, the right to self-governance, and the rights of ecosystems. It then prohibited commercial natural gas extraction within the city as an activity which would inherently violate those civil and environmental rights.

32. Communities, for instance, often turn to zoning laws to stop unwanted projects. Zoning laws, however, while created to designate certain areas for certain uses, were never intended to prohibit uses permitted by the state or federal government. Using zoning laws to bar a legal use within a municipality runs afoul of constitutional protections provided to the proposer of the use—with the proposers of most major uses being development and other corporations.

33. Given the current legal landscape, it is inevitable that many local laws will be declared unconstitutional. However, given the frame of these laws—advancing a local expansion of the rights of people, communities, and nature via localized bills of rights—and the lack of any contemporary jurisprudence on municipal expansion of rights, the laws may well represent a new, cutting-edge form of activism that may survive some judicial challenges. Local laws hewn by the judicial axe have value under this organizing structure—as educational vehicles which illustrate how the current system functions.

34. According to historian Pauline Maier, in her book *American Scripture: Making the Declaration of Independence*, during the late colonial-era communities including towns, counties, boroughs, and what we would generally call *municipalities* today advanced over ninety declarations of independence, which eventually were distilled into the historic federal document we remember.
35. Those local constitutions already have begun to emerge in places like Pittsburgh, Pennsylvania, and Spokane, Washington, where new bills of rights have been drafted and adopted, or included in proposed ballot initiatives. Those rights include the right to vibrant local economies, preventive healthcare, and affordable housing, along with workplace and ecosystem rights.
36. The ordinance creates a food bill of rights and then prohibits those activities within the municipality that would violate those rights. Those prohibited activities include corporate farming, the use of sewage sludge, and the cultivation of genetically modified seeds.
37. Tellingly, the 2009 and 2011 initiative drew opposition from both corporate interests and some progressive organizations. Business interests claimed that the initiative would bankrupt the city and drive corporate employers out of Spokane; progressive organizations claimed that the initiative was "too much, too soon," and several key progressives campaigned against it. It should be noted that both the Abolitionists and the Suffragists ran into similar opposition—the Abolitionists from the American Colonization Society, which worked to send freed slaves to African colonies, and the Suffragists from the National American Woman Suffrage Association, which worked through conventional congressional lobbying toward eventual suffrage.
38. One school of thought holds that unless states provide constitutional change mechanisms for the people of the state to exercise directly, that legislatively-constricted constitutional change violates the constitutional right of the people of the state to local, community self-government. That situation could lead to a class action lawsuit filed against the state for violation of that right.
39. Any constitutional changes, to be legitimate, must be proposed by the communities who have been blueprinting constitutional changes through the passage of local ordinances and home rule charters. Accordingly, these draft amendments are offered only to frame the major concepts that must be addressed within any constitutional change if

that change is intended to "legalize" municipal authority toward sustainability.
40. This is a situation that has arisen before in American politics in numerous places where the existing system has refused to give way to necessary societal changes. Many would argue that such changes are the right of the populace to make if the state operates in such a way to violate those rights on a wide-scale basis. Indeed, such is the very foundation of the Declaration of Independence, when it envisioned altering or abolishing those forms of government that become destructive of rights.
41. It also raises questions beyond the scope of this pamphlet, such as whether sustainability and local democracy are possible in the face of power exercised by the centralized authority of a U.S. Supreme Court or Senate. A process to rewrite the U.S. Constitution must eventually consider whether the institutions which have gotten us to this place must be replaced with other institutions created by different values and interests.
42. Given the existing structure of constitutional law, long-term structural change is the only avenue that offers a different, viable future for both human and natural communities. Activism focused on short-term change which is delinked from leveraging long-term structural change not only fails to fix the underlying problem, it exacerbates the situation by giving credence to the myth that conventional activism is sufficient to remedy the structural problems. Only activism aimed at replacing minorities of corporate decision-makers with community majorities holds the promise of achieving economic and environmental sustainability.

About the Community Environmental Legal Defense Fund

The Community Environmental Legal Defense Fund (CELDF) is bringing public interest law and grassroots organizing together in a unique legal and organizing strategy to build a movement for *Community Rights and the Rights of Nature.*

Founded in 1995, CELDF has assisted close to two hundred communities across the country to ban shale gas drilling and fracking, factory farming, sewage sludging of farmland, water privatization, and other threats through *first-in-the-nation "community rights" laws.*

Those laws establish rights of people, communities, and nature, while prohibiting activities—such as fracking—which would violate those rights. Those laws include the *first communities in the U.S. to legally recognize nature and ecosystems as possessing independently enforceable rights.*

As corporate constitutional "rights" and other legal doctrines—including the preemption of community decision making by state and federal government—stand in the way of local self-governance and sustainability, CELDF's work with communities necessarily challenges those doctrines. With CELDF's help, communities across the country are now directly challenging those doctrines by asserting a constitutional right to local, community self-government.

As CELDF's work has expanded in the U.S., it has also broadened to include work in Ecuador, Nepal, India, Australia, Canada, and other countries. This work included assisting the Ecuador Constituent Assembly to draft the *world's first rights of nature constitutional provisions*, which were approved by popular referendum in 2008.

Community Environmental Legal Defense Fund
P.O. Box 360
Mercersburg, PA 17236
(717) 498-0054
http://www.celdf.org
info@celdf.org

 PM Press was founded at the end of 2007 by a small collection of folks with decades of publishing, media, and organizing experience. PM Press co-conspirators have published and distributed hundreds of books, pamphlets, CDs, and DVDs. Members of PM have founded enduring book fairs, spearheaded victorious tenant organizing campaigns, and worked closely with bookstores, academic conferences, and even rock bands to deliver political and challenging ideas to all walks of life. We're old enough to know what we're doing and young enough to know what's at stake.

We seek to create radical and stimulating fiction and non-fiction books, pamphlets, T-shirts, visual and audio materials to entertain, educate, and inspire you. We aim to distribute these through every available channel with every available technology, whether that means you are seeing anarchist classics at our bookfair stalls; reading our latest vegan cookbook at the café; downloading geeky fiction e-books; or digging new music and timely videos from our website.

PM Press is always on the lookout for talented and skilled volunteers, artists, activists, and writers to work with. If you have a great idea for a project or can contribute in some way, please get in touch.

PM Press
PO Box 23912
Oakland CA 94623
510-658-3906
www.pmpress.org

Friends of PM

These are indisputably momentous times—the financial system is melting down globally and the Empire is stumbling. Now more than ever there is a vital need for radical ideas.

In the eight years since its founding—and on a mere shoestring—PM Press has risen to the formidable challenge of publishing and distributing knowledge and entertainment for the struggles ahead. With hundreds of releases to date, we have published an impressive and stimulating array of literature, art, music, politics, and culture. Using every available medium, we've succeeded in connecting those hungry for ideas and information to those putting them into practice.

Friends of PM allows you to directly help impact, amplify, and revitalize the discourse and actions of radical writers, filmmakers, and artists. It provides us with a stable foundation from which we can build upon our early successes and provides a much-needed subsidy for the materials that can't necessarily pay their own way. You can help make that happen—and receive every new title automatically delivered to your door once a month—by joining as a Friend of PM Press. And, we'll throw in a free T-Shirt when you sign up.

Here are your options:
- $30 a month: Get all books and pamphlets plus 50% discount on all webstore purchases
- $40 a month: Get all PM Press releases plus 50% discount on all webstore purchases
- $100 a month: Superstar—Everything plus PM merchandise, free downloads, and 50% discount on all webstore purchases

For those who can't afford $30 or more a month, we're introducing **Sustainer Rates** at $15, $10 and $5. Sustainers get a free PM Press T-Shirt and a 50% discount on all purchases from our website.

Your Visa or Mastercard will be billed once a month, until you tell us to stop. Or until our efforts succeed in bringing the revolution around. Or the financial meltdown of Capital makes plastic redundant. Whichever comes first.